THE MOON OF THE
MOUNTAIN
LIONS

THE THIRTEEN MOONS

The Moon of the Owls (JANUARY)

The Moon of the Bears (FEBRUARY)

The Moon of the Salamanders (MARCH)

The Moon of the Chickarees (APRIL)

The Moon of the Monarch Butterflies (MAY)

The Moon of the Fox Pups (JUNE)

The Moon of the Wild Pigs (JULY)

The Moon of the Mountain Lions (AUGUST)

The Moon of the Deer (SEPTEMBER)

The Moon of the Alligators (OCTOBER)

The Moon of the Gray Wolves (NOVEMBER)

The Moon of the Winter Bird (DECEMBER)

The Moon of the Moles (DECEMBER–JANUARY)

NEW EDITION   THE THIRTEEN MOONS

THE MOON OF THE
MOUNTAIN
LIONS

BY JEAN CRAIGHEAD GEORGE
ILLUSTRATED BY RON PARKER

HarperCollins*Publishers*

Juv.

QL 795. P85 G4 1991

The illustrations in this book were
painted with designer's gouache
on watercolor board.

The Moon of the Mountain Lions
Text copyright © 1969, 1991 by Jean Craighead George
Illustrations copyright © 1991 by R.S. Parker

All rights reserved. No part of this book may be used or reproduced
in any manner whatsoever without written permission except in the
case of brief quotations embodied in critical articles and reviews.
Printed in the United States of America. For information address
HarperCollins Children's Books, a division of HarperCollins
Publishers, 10 East 53rd Street, New York, NY 10022.
Typography by Al Cetta
2 3 4 5 6 7 8 9 10
NEW EDITION

Library of Congress Cataloging-in-Publication Data
George, Jean Craighead, date
    The moon of the mountain lions / by Jean Craighead George ;
illustrated by Ron Parker. — New ed.
        p.   cm. — (The Thirteen moons)
    Includes bibliographical references and index.
    Summary: Describes the experiences of a young mountain lion
during the month of August in his natural habitat on the side of Mount
Olympus, in Washington State.
    ISBN 0-06-022429-0. — ISBN 0-06-022438-X (lib. bdg.)
    1. Pumas—Juvenile literature.   2. Pumas—Washington (State)
—Olympic Mountains—Juvenile literature. [1. Pumas.] I. Parker,
Ron, ill. II. Title. III. Series: George, Jean Craighead, date.
Thirteen moons (HarperCollins)
QL795.P85G4   1991   90-39451
599.74′428—dc20   CIP
                                                            AC

Why is this series called The Thirteen Moons?

Each year there are either thirteen full moons or thirteen new moons. This series of books is named in their honor.

Our culture, which bases its calendar on sun-time, has no names for the thirteen moons. I have named the thirteen lunar months after thirteen North American animals. Primarily night prowlers, these animals, at a particular time of the year in a particular place, do wondrous things. The places are known to you, but the animal moon names are not because I made them up. So that you can place them on our sun calendar, I have identified them with the names of our months. When I ran out of these, I gave the thirteenth moon, the Moon of the Moles, the expandable name December-January.

Fortunately, the animals do not need calendars, for names or no names, sun-time or moon-time, they follow their own inner clocks.

—JEAN CRAIGHEAD GEORGE

THE YOUNG MOUNTAIN LION
opened his mouth and rolled out his tongue in
a waking yawn. Lying in his summer den at
timberline, he turned his gaze upon his home
on the side of Mount Olympus in Washington.
Snowcapped peaks speared the darkness above
him. An alpine meadow splattered with flowers
lay below, and far down the mountain shaggy
forests hugged the slopes and glacial valleys.
Below them the northern rain forest reached to
the Pacific Ocean.

Stretching and cupping his whiskers forward,
the noble cat arose and quietly stepped into the

moonlight. He stood beneath the moon of August, the moon of change.

The hummingbirds, sippers of flower nectar, had already sensed the force of this moon. They were ready to migrate. The temperature had dropped only one or two degrees across North America and had actually risen that much on the Pacific Coast, yet the flower birds were ready to go. The sun was setting earlier and rising later. The days were growing shorter. Snow and darkness were coming to the mountains.

At the dawn of this day several male rufous hummingbirds, some of the tiniest birds in the world, had darted past the lion's den as they spun south on whirling wings. No bigger than daisy heads, they were off toward winter homes on the plateaus of Mexico three thousand miles away. Their females stayed behind to hurriedly feed the last brood of nestlings. They would see their bud-sized youngsters out of the nests and onto their wings, teach them how to sip the nectar of the last lilies and bellflowers, then all would follow the males to the sunny winter lands where flowers bloomed.

The swallows also felt the change of the August moon. Great flocks were gathering by the thousands and tens of thousands over lakes, marshes, and seacoasts. Almost always on the wing, these agile birds have tiny, feeble feet that they rarely use. Before the moon would wane they would climb high into the sky and, out of sight of man and beast, circle and rest on their wings. Then, on a cue from the sun, they would turn south and speed away. The next day the swallows would be gone, leaving the skies strangely empty, like beaches when winter comes.

Other animals were responding differently to the change. In the deserts, on the August-dry prairies, and in forests from Mexico up through Canada, the chipmunks, toads, and frogs were asleep. This was not the sleep of hibernation but of estivation, summer's torpor. In this quiet state these animals were avoiding the adversities of the month, dryness and heat.

One beast, however would combine the sleeps of summer and winter. In the rockslides, the Olympic marmots, the whistlers of high country, were getting ready for the longest sleep of all the mammals—the nine months from mid-August to mid-May. Some of the marmots were already taking naps that lasted a day or two. Fat and drowsy, they slept longer and longer with each snooze. As they did so, their hearts beat more slowly and their bodies cooled. Eventually they would not be able to awaken until spring. Those that were still running across the rockslides whistled to each other, like children calling their dogs.

The lion tasted the wind with his tongue and nose. It tasted of another change, the change of aging and ripening. The wind bore the scent of sweet huckleberries, ripe gooseberries, and twin-berries. This change did not interest the mountain lion, for he was a meat eater, or carnivore. Having looked, smelled, and tasted, the young lion now listened. He rotated his ears. The elk and deer had changed their direction. They were no longer climbing among the peaks but were moving downward. He heard them snapping branches in the forest below.

Since spring they had been wandering upward toward the alpine meadows as the melting snow uncovered sweet grasses. Now the grasses were dying, the growing season of the high country was ending and like the birds, the deer and elk were on migration. Their migration, however, was not south but down the mountain, and this concerned the lion. The deer and elk were his staff of life. He had moved up the mountain with them in the spring, harvesting the weak and infirm as he went. At about five thousand feet above sea level, where the trees stopped and the rocks, ice, and alpine prairies took over, the young lion had denned for the summer. His shelter was a twisted thicket of alpine firs, the last trees to withstand the driving wind and stunting cold at the tops of the mountains. They mark the timberline beyond which no trees grow.

Tonight the elk and deer were two thousand feet below the lion in a lower and, therefore, different kind of forest. On mountains the forests change with the altitude, the tougher trees braving the rugged heights. The lion could smell the pungent cedars the herds were trampling lower down the mountain. He must follow.

Before he entered the forest, he stopped in the last alpine meadow and tipped his ears forward. An elk had injured his foot in a crevasse several days ago and was limping through the trees, *da, thump, thump, thump*. The lion swished his tail. This animal was wounded. In the scheme of things he would falter and eventually be harvested.

Slowly the lion crossed the meadow. Beneath his feet a different sort of change was taking place. Spring was beginning. Under the leaf stems of the tiny alpine willow trees, no taller than a thumb, new buds were forming. This was happening not only on the mountain but all across the northern United States and Canada. Next year's willows, elm, maple, beech, and apple leaf buds were forming. As they emerged, the cells that brought food and water to the old leaves shut down. When these were sealed off, the leaves would lose their chlorophyll, turn yellow, red, orange, or gold and fall to the ground.

The young lion stopped at the edge of the forest and listened. He had lost sight and sound of the limping elk, so he climbed a leaning cedar to search for him. Lean and muscular, the lion was magnificently beautiful. Tawny in color, he had black smudges under his eyes and along his nose. His back was as straight as a leveling rod, his paws immense. His tail was tipped with black and almost as long as he. It touched the ground and curled up at the end. He weighed more than two hundred pounds. He was a cougar, or mountain lion, of North America. Almost as large as African lions, cougars are the second largest species of cat in the New World. Only jaguars surpass them in length and weight.

A hundred years ago mountain lions were abundant in all the mountains of the United States and Canada. Now they are rare in the United States and found only in the lonely wilderness areas of the West, Southwest, and Florida. Washington's Olympic Peninsula, a land barely touched by humans, still has its appropriate number of mountain lions. Because of their presence the elk and deer do not become so numerous that they ravage trees, bushes, grasses, and the wildlife that depend on them for shelter and food. The lions keep the herds in balance with their environment.

From the tree, the young lion could see the Hoh River valley where he had been born and raised. Turning his head he glanced up the mountain. The snow-covered peaks of the Olympic Mountains shone like silver saw blades against the purple-black sky. In the moonlight the mountain glaciers looked like Rocky Mountain goats sleeping on the dark rocks. Some of the spots may even have been goats. The goats lived at timberline and above all year round.

The lion's sensitive ears could hear the largest glacier, Blue Glacier, moan as its tons of ice moved great boulders, slowly grinding them to dust. In the August heat, all sixty glaciers were melting. The melt spilled down the mountain, forming waterfalls, streams, and the many rivers that joined the sea.

The lion could not locate the lame elk. Silently he leaped to the ground and slipped into the forest.

Born three years ago under the August moon— lion cubs in the north arrive in spring and into the summer—the young lion had lived with his mother and two sisters in a high valley of the Hoh River. He rarely saw his father, who had remained with his mother only a short time before returning to his solitary life. He would seek out the young lion's mother again in two or three years, when the cubs were on their own. Meanwhile, like most cats, he would live alone.

After a three-month pregnancy the lioness had given birth to cubs who were about one foot long and covered with spotted fur. In ten days their eyes opened.

They were weaned in three months. By that time the young lion had shed the spots and ringed tail of his childhood. He weighed about forty pounds and ventured out of the rock den with his mother and sisters. Together they hunted around the den, catching grouse, rabbits, and occasionally a coyote. When they were almost fully grown, they hunted farther and farther afield until they knew all about the game in their kingdom of several square miles. Eventually they were able to hunt the prey of the adult mountain lion—deer and elk. Each dawn they returned to their den.

At home they rolled and played like house cats, batting stones and flowers around, jumping on each other. Like house cats they also made many sounds, expressing different feelings.

A year ago in July the young lion had left home. He climbed out of the valley, following the deer and elk up through tall forests, over rocks, and along cliffs. After several days he came to an alpine meadow high up on Mount Olympus where the herds grazed. No other lion ran him off

the rich find, so he stayed in a twisted alpine fir forest until the moon of change drove the herds down-mountain. He went with them down almost to sea level, where the stately northern rain forests grow. Here the herds and the young lion lived all winter in a forest kept forever green by the warm rains from the sea.

One night in spring a thrilling sound brought him to his feet. A female mountain lion was calling from the other side of the Hoh River. Her scream was the high-pitched cry that the young lion recognized to be a mother cat's danger call to her cubs. He sat down and stared at the far side of the river. His whiskers stood out straight and his tail swished in anticipation.

The thin cry of a lost cub came from the riverbed. The young lion did not move. A stick snapped across the river. A lioness and two cubs slipped out from among the alder trees at the river edge and ran toward the water. The cubs were both males. The mother meowed and the lost cub ran to meet them. This one was a

female—a lively cub of almost a year, who piqued the interest of the young lion. He watched her closely.

After the family was reunited, the mother led them to a log. The cubs sat down. The mother lay on her side and, reaching under the fallen tree with her strong paws, pulled out some game she had cached there. The cubs set upon it with snarls and growls. When their stomachs were round with food, the mother shoved the leftovers back under the log and, kicking leaves over it, led her tawny-colored youngsters into the eerie yellow-green forest. The young lion watched until they disappeared.

After that he was constantly on the alert for the family. Twice he heard the mother call and several times he saw the cubs. They were growing up. Their tumbles and rollicks became skilled pounces. Their thin cries developed into growls and roars. One night in June, he heard the lioness call from the northern end of her kingdom, and he saw the family no more. It was time for him to follow the elk and deer up the mountain.

Now, two months later, the moon of change was rising. The young lion was headed down-mountain again. As he went, like all cats, he climbed logs and rocks and cliffs to survey the land below. Having lost track of the limping elk, he strode to the top of a cliff to search for him. Rocks avalanched below him and once more he heard the *da, thump, thump, thump* of the limping buck. Dropping from the cliff like plunging water, he struck the earth and tracked the elk to the edge of a small lake, where he lost him. Around the lake grew bluebells, yarrow, glacier lilies, cinquefoil, and cow parsnips. They were all blooming at once. In the lowlands some of these are spring flowers, while others are fall flowers, but in the mountains the growing season is so short that everything must bloom and go to seed between June and September. Spring's bluebells come into flower with autumn's asters.

As the lion walked around the lake, he awakened a junco who was sleeping behind a curtain of moss beneath an embankment. The bird saw the lion's

shadow in the moonlight and called *tik-tik*, the danger signal of the junco. Her five youngsters, sleeping under roots and flowers nearby, awakened. They did not fly, for their mother's note warned them to tighten their feet on their perches and sit perfectly still.

The youngsters had been flying for only three days. Nevertheless, they knew where the seeds of the alpine flowers lay, and today they had learned to shell them. Tomorrow they would bathe and preen their feathers and the next day they would sun themselves, the last achievement of a baby bird before its adolescence. Then they would start down the mountain with the elk, the deer, and the lion. They would not spend much time with them, however. When the snows came they would migrate to the lowlands of British Columbia and even as far as Mexico. Everywhere they would be known affectionately as "snowbirds," as their white tail feathers flashed over cold gray fields and under bird feeders in backyards.

The mother junco watched a starlike avalanche

lily bounce above her head. When it became still, she waited and then softly called "all's well" to her family. The enemy was gone.

The young lion walked to the spillway where the lake poured over its embankment to become a stream. The stream rushed downhill forming waterfalls and pools. He listened, but the limping elk could not be heard over the sound of water. He continued down among mountain hemlocks, silver and Alaska firs, and gigantic red cedars. Pine drops and twinberries grew under these trees.

In silence the lion searched for the limping elk, who was aware of the hunter and was hiding in a dense clump of cedars not far from the lion. Sensing him, the lion climbed to a high ledge. The limping elk saw him outlined against the sky. Terrified, he dashed down-mountain to a stream at the foot of a waterfall. So soft was the floor of the forest that the lion did not hear him go.

A most remarkable bird heard the elk splash into the water. He was a dipper, or water ouzel, a small gray songbird. He peered out from behind a waterfall, where he was roosting in an air pocket, and shifted his weight from one foot to the other. He had flown there at dusk through a split in the falling water. Dippers are birds of rushing streams and falling cascades. Wild water is their home. Dry and well hidden, the wondrous bird preened his feathers until they lay so smoothly no water could seep in, then went back to sleep.

The dipper had hatched in a round nest of moss on the wall of the gorge above the cascade. He had remained there for three weeks—a long time for a songbird, which usually remains in the nest only ten to twelve days. But the longer the dipper stayed in the nest, the stronger he became. He needed to be strong because he had to fly from his nest across the raging cascade. Two weeks ago he had made the perilous flight.

Although he had landed safely and was exhausted, his parents would not let him rest. They led him right into the stream. Surprisingly, he floated on the water like a duck. His parents demonstrated how to use the swift currents to cross the raging torrent without being washed away. When he had succeeded, they led him to a quiet pool. They dove and swam underwater. The young bird hesitated, then dove. As silver bubbles passed his eyes, he instinctively pumped his wings and arrived on the bottom of the stream. There he grasped pebbles with the hooklike claws on his toes, and ran along the stream bottom. His parents gobbled the larvae of the black fly and so did the young dipper. Surfacing with them, he flew through the air and alit beside his parents on a ledge behind the cascade. There in an air pocket he rested, safe from hawk, bass, and weasel.

This night the young dipper was on his own, independent of his parents. Through the falling water he saw the young lion come to the stream. The bird was not afraid. He looked at the big cat, then stuck his beak in his feathers. Not even a mountain lion would dare to walk into the thunderous waterfall.

The lion saw the elk splash out of the stream. With a bound he followed.

Above the mountain lion, high up in the fir trees that lined the stream, slept the tiny birds of the treetops, the kinglets. They were waiting for September, when they would follow the hummingbirds south. Pine siskins, which would fly south as far as the snowbirds do, were asleep against the boles of tall trees. These small birds were of little interest to the lion. He was, however, interested in the sweet odor of the blue grouse sleeping at the edge of a cedar glen. These grouse of the Olympic Peninsula were tasty food. He crouched to catch one, but did not. The lame elk was crossing the stream again. The lion followed it downhill in deliberate pursuit.

Leaping the waterway, he ran quite a distance, then suddenly slowed down and stopped. A bull elk was pawing the ground and thrashing his huge antlers in a grassy glade. He was alone, preparing for the mating season. In September he would bugle like the monarch elk he was and call his harem to him. And he would fight all bulls who dared to come near.

The lion twisted his ears and sniffed. A large herd of elk was in a clearing above him. They were resting and browsing as they slowly worked their way down the Hoh Valley. The lion was about to stop and join their more leisurely ascent when he heard the limping elk. He was hobbling down the mountain in great fear. The lion pursued him down an elk trail and into the mysteriously beautiful northern rain forest. Here the huge Sitka spruce, western hemlock, and Douglas fir were two hundred and fifty feet tall. Their trunks were six to nine feet in diameter, and many of the trees were five hundred years old. Water-loving mosses, mushrooms, ferns, vines, and microbes grew in luxurious profusion. The lion stopped and listened. The moist vegetation hushed the forest.

He could not hear the elk. The elk was tired, and was standing only a few hundred feet away. Thirst assailed the lion, and he walked to a spring to drink. Tiny frogs, which had just emerged from their tadpole stage and come onto the land, felt his step. They leaped back into the water.

Waves from their dives knocked against the lion's nose. Unwittingly a large frog hopped onto his paw, then jumped ashore. It crawled up a fern and clung there by means of the suction pads on its feet. The lion turned his head to observe it. The frog plunged back into the spring.

The lion was about to drink when he saw beside his other paw another amphibian—a northwestern hop toad. She, too, had become an adult this month. The lion lifted his paw. The toad jumped, not into the spring like the frog, but toward the woods. After spending months in the spring the toad had changed from a water-loving pollywog into a land creature. The lion reached for her playfully. The toad leaped four feet and disappeared.

Sniffing the air, the lion picked up the scent of the lame elk, now moving away. He followed him along the stream that flowed from the spring.

A great splashing in the shallows caught his attention. A large coho salmon was fighting his way, half out of water, toward a gravel bar. It was the same gravel bar where he had hatched. Now, seven years later, he was coming back to it. He had swum from the deep ocean up the Hoh River, to the feeder stream, and finally to the gravel bar where he had started his life. Here he would spawn with one of the females who were also coming home to this bar. Together the salmon would spawn and die, the last deeds of these coho salmon and millions more like them.

The lion left the salmon and followed the scent of the lame elk.

The moon was low in the western sky. Dawn would soon follow. A killdeer awoke beside the stream and flew screaming into the darkness. The lion ignored her. His hunger was beginning to gnaw at him. He wanted the elk. He climbed to the top of a bluff and saw him directly below. Crouching to pounce, he took aim.

He did not leap. Across the river something moved. Among the skyscrapers of Sitka spruce, a shadow flitted in such harmony with the forest that only the night vision of a cat could tell who walked there. A surge of warmth rushed over him. He forgot his hunger. Down the top of the cliff on the other side of the river came the child lioness and her mother. Behind them strolled one brother.

He tensed. Coming toward the family on the same trail was an enormous black bear. His head was low, his shoulder blades pumping up and down. He marched with great strength and deliberation.

Before the young lion's eyes the mother lioness and bear met. Both were surprised. Both reacted. The lioness extended her razor-sharp claws, hissed, and leaped for the bear's neck. The bear reared to his hind feet, swung his powerful front paw, and tore open the back of the lioness. He locked his teeth in her shoulder and, as he did, lost his footing on the edge of the cliff. He fell, dragging the lioness with him to the river shore forty feet below. Although they pawed at trees and branches, they could not break their plunge. They crashed to the earth. A long silence followed.

Presently the bear rolled to his feet and limped away. The lioness did not get up.

With three bounds the young lion crossed the river to the lifeless cat. He caterwauled, a lonesome, bloodcurdling scream.

A leaf, as large as a dinner plate and yellow with the change of August, fell from the top of the cliff. The big maple leaf spiraled to the ground. The young lion looked up. Peering over the edge of the cliff was the child lioness. He called to her. Slowly she came down the trail on the rim of the cliff and stopped before him. He sniffed her ears and nose. They rubbed foreheads in greeting, then he led her into the rain forest.

The child lioness stayed close to the young lion's heels. Not far behind them, moving with hesitation, came the yearling brother. The young lion had a family. The orphans followed him as they had followed their mother, creating a new role for a solitary male mountain lion.

The three walked deeper into the forest. Where the trees made columned hallways, the child lioness took the lead. She led the young lion and her brother under the roots of fallen spruce, upholstered in soft club moss. She led them into a glade where lacy ferns grew everywhere—on trees, rocks, limbs, other ferns. She took them over a forest floor bright green with oxalis—a pretty wood sorrel that provides a carpet of three-leafed designs.

The child lioness led them to the foot of a moss-covered boulder. Leaping onto it, she turned and looked down at the young lion. He vaulted to her side. She crept under an enormous log covered with ferns and fragrant bedstraw. There she lay down. The brother climbed up the rock and stretched out beside her. They were home.

Lowering himself to his belly, shoulders and haunches jutting, head erect, the young lion sat sphinxlike on the rock and stared at the child lioness and her brother, not knowing quite what to do about them.

The young lion dozed in the quiet time just before dawn when the night animals are bedding down and the day animals are not yet up. He did not see the monkey flowers bob in the wind that stirs as the day breaks. He did not see the ferns absorb dew, or the wind pick up their spores and carry them away to drop and plant them. Nor did he hear the winter wren sing his morning song.

Exuberant little birds, the wrens are permanent residents of the northern rain forest. They do not migrate like the hummingbirds and swallows but stay in this environment all year. The wren sang only briefly, for it was August, and the singing and nesting seasons were over. He flew off to eat, paying no attention to the lions or the far-off drilling of a pileated woodpecker, a two-foot-high bird who was a match for the enormous trees of the rain forest.

A chickaree, a little red squirrel, scolded and announced the passing of a bobcat, a cat about a third the size of the young lion. A raven sneaked through the trees on her way to the coast to hunt mice. Then the sun came up and the lions briefly opened their eyes.

They purred to each other and went to sleep.

Dull swishing sounds in the forest marked the homecoming of a herd of black-tailed deer. As the sun came up, they bedded down for the day. Deer feed in the predawn and at twilight. They sleep in the bright daylight and during the dark of night.

All day the lions slept, occasionally waking and purring to each other. The sun shone—a rare event in this land where ten to twelve feet of rain falls in the course of a year.

At sundown the mountain lions got to their feet. The child lioness leaped from the boulder and ran down the family trail that led to the ocean. The young lion followed. Suddenly he crouched. There was a flash of movement, and a thud. The lion had felled a deer for his family. They dined, then proceeded leisurely toward the ocean.

When the moon had waxed from a sliver to ball and waned from ball to a sliver, the three lions reached the ocean. Curious about the sea and sky, they walked the beach until the sun came up and

drove them back to the shelter of the forest.

The young lion was weary of his kittens. He turned and walked away. Inland along a riverbed the first of the elk had gathered for the winter. He climbed a toppled tree six feet in diameter, waited and watched. Alone and content, he lounged in the feathery mosses and deer ferns.

The winter rainy season was upon the forest, the fog dense, and the plants dripping like chimes. He heard the child lioness call from close by. He waited. Presently she stole quietly out of the yellow-green forest and sat down on the far end of his log. He tucked his paws under his chest and stared at her. She tucked her paws under her chest and stared at him. They looked away, then back again. All night they stared and looked away.

In the darkness before dawn the lion yawned and went to hunt. The lioness arose and walked up the riverbank. Each looked back at the other. The courtship of the mountain lion had begun.

The moon of change had brought the young lion a mate.

Bibliography

Audubon, John James, and the Rev. John Bachman, D.C. *The Imperial Collection of Audubon Animals*. Maplewood, N.J.: Hammond, Inc., 1967.

Gray, Robert. *Cougar, the Natural Life of a North American Mountain Lion*. New York: Grosset, 1972.

Macdonald, David, ed. *The Encyclopedia of Mammals*. New York: Facts on File Inc., 1984.

McDearmon, Kay. *Cougar*. New York: Dodd Mead, 1977.

Palmer, Ralph S., *The Mammal Guide*. Garden City, N.Y.: Doubleday & Company, 1954.

Rumsey, Marian. *Lion on the Run*. New York: Morrow, 1973.

Wallace, Bill. *Shadow on the Snow*. New York: Holiday House, 1985.

Index